[*Swimming* Log Book]

This book belongs to

👤	
📞	
✉	
📍	
✏	

Training Log 2

Notes 102

Log Start Date : _____

Date		Beginner ○	Intermediate ○	Advanced ○
Time				

WARM UP

Activity	Distance	Reps	Time	Rest

SETS

Activity	Distance	Reps	Time	Rest

COOL DOWN

Activity	Distance	Reps	Time	Rest

TOTAL				

Date	
Time	

Beginner ◯   Intermediate ◯   Advanced ◯

WARM UP

Activity	Distance	Reps	Time	Rest

SETS

Activity	Distance	Reps	Time	Rest

COOL DOWN

Activity	Distance	Reps	Time	Rest

TOTAL				

Date	
Time	

Beginner ○   Intermediate ○   Advanced ○

WARM UP				
Activity	Distance	Reps	Time	Rest

		SETS		
Activity	Distance	Reps	Time	Rest

		COOL DOWN		
Activity	Distance	Reps	Time	Rest

TOTAL				

Date	
Time	

Beginner ○   Intermediate ○   Advanced ○

WARM UP				
Activity	Distance	Reps	Time	Rest

	SETS			
Activity	Distance	Reps	Time	Rest

		COOL DOWN		
Activity	Distance	Reps	Time	Rest

TOTAL				

Date		Beginner ○	Intermediate ○	Advanced ○
Time				

WARM UP

Activity	Distance	Reps	Time	Rest

SETS

Activity	Distance	Reps	Time	Rest

COOL DOWN

Activity	Distance	Reps	Time	Rest

TOTAL				

Date	
Time	

Beginner ○   Intermediate ○   Advanced ○

WARM UP	Activity	Distance	Reps	Time	Rest

SETS	Activity	Distance	Reps	Time	Rest

COOL DOWN	Activity	Distance	Reps	Time	Rest

TOTAL				

Date		Beginner ○	Intermediate ○	Advanced ○
Time				

WARM UP				
Activity	Distance	Reps	Time	Rest

SETS				
Activity	Distance	Reps	Time	Rest

COOL DOWN				
Activity	Distance	Reps	Time	Rest

TOTAL				

Date	
Time	

Beginner ○   Intermediate ○   Advanced ○

WARM UP				
Activity	Distance	Reps	Time	Rest

		SETS		
Activity	Distance	Reps	Time	Rest

			COOL DOWN	
Activity	Distance	Reps	Time	Rest

TOTAL				

9

| Date | | Beginner ◯ | Intermediate ◯ | Advanced ◯ |
| Time | | | | |

WARM UP				
Activity	Distance	Reps	Time	Rest

SETS				
Activity	Distance	Reps	Time	Rest

COOL DOWN				
Activity	Distance	Reps	Time	Rest

TOTAL				

Date	
Time	

Beginner ○   Intermediate ○   Advanced ○

WARM UP

Activity	Distance	Reps	Time	Rest

SETS

Activity	Distance	Reps	Time	Rest

COOL DOWN

Activity	Distance	Reps	Time	Rest

TOTAL				

Date		Beginner ◯	Intermediate ◯	Advanced ◯
Time				

WARM UP

Activity	Distance	Reps	Time	Rest

SETS

Activity	Distance	Reps	Time	Rest

COOL DOWN

Activity	Distance	Reps	Time	Rest

TOTAL				

Date	
Time	

Beginner ○   Intermediate ○   Advanced ○

WARM UP				
Activity	Distance	Reps	Time	Rest

SETS				
Activity	Distance	Reps	Time	Rest

COOL DOWN				
Activity	Distance	Reps	Time	Rest

TOTAL				

Date		Beginner ○	Intermediate ○	Advanced ○
Time				

WARM UP

Activity	Distance	Reps	Time	Rest

SETS

Activity	Distance	Reps	Time	Rest

COOL DOWN

Activity	Distance	Reps	Time	Rest

TOTAL				

Date	
Time	

Beginner ○   Intermediate ○   Advanced ○

WARM UP				
Activity	Distance	Reps	Time	Rest

SETS				
Activity	Distance	Reps	Time	Rest

		COOL DOWN		
Activity	Distance	Reps	Time	Rest

TOTAL				

Date	
Time	

Beginner ○   Intermediate ○   Advanced ○

WARM UP				
Activity	Distance	Reps	Time	Rest

SETS				
Activity	Distance	Reps	Time	Rest

COOL DOWN				
Activity	Distance	Reps	Time	Rest

TOTAL				

Date	
Time	

Beginner ○   Intermediate ○   Advanced ○

WARM UP				
Activity	Distance	Reps	Time	Rest

SETS				
Activity	Distance	Reps	Time	Rest

COOL DOWN				
Activity	Distance	Reps	Time	Rest

TOTAL				

Date	
Time	

Beginner ◯　　Intermediate ◯　　Advanced ◯

WARM UP	Distance	Reps	Time	Rest
Activity	Distance	Reps	Time	Rest

SETS	Distance	Reps	Time	Rest
Activity	Distance	Reps	Time	Rest

		COOL DOWN		
Activity	Distance	Reps	Time	Rest

TOTAL				

Date	
Time	

Beginner ◯   Intermediate ◯   Advanced ◯

WARM UP

Activity	Distance	Reps	Time	Rest

SETS

Activity	Distance	Reps	Time	Rest

COOL DOWN

Activity	Distance	Reps	Time	Rest

TOTAL				

Date	
Time	

Beginner ◯   Intermediate ◯   Advanced ◯

WARM UP				
Activity	Distance	Reps	Time	Rest

	SETS			
Activity	Distance	Reps	Time	Rest

		COOL DOWN		
Activity	Distance	Reps	Time	Rest

TOTAL				

Date	
Time	

Beginner ◯ Intermediate ◯ Advanced ◯

WARM UP

Activity	Distance	Reps	Time	Rest

SETS

Activity	Distance	Reps	Time	Rest

COOL DOWN

Activity	Distance	Reps	Time	Rest

TOTAL				

Date	
Time	

Beginner ⃝   Intermediate ⃝   Advanced ⃝

WARM UP				
Activity	Distance	Reps	Time	Rest

SETS				
Activity	Distance	Reps	Time	Rest

COOL DOWN				
Activity	Distance	Reps	Time	Rest

TOTAL				

Date	
Time	

Beginner ○   Intermediate ○   Advanced ○

WARM UP				
Activity	Distance	Reps	Time	Rest

SETS				
Activity	Distance	Reps	Time	Rest

COOL DOWN				
Activity	Distance	Reps	Time	Rest

TOTAL				

Date		Beginner ○	Intermediate ○	Advanced ○
Time				

WARM UP

Activity	Distance	Reps	Time	Rest

SETS

Activity	Distance	Reps	Time	Rest

COOL DOWN

Activity	Distance	Reps	Time	Rest

TOTAL				

| Date | | Beginner ○ | Intermediate ○ | Advanced ○ |
| Time | | | | |

WARM UP				
Activity	Distance	Reps	Time	Rest

SETS				
Activity	Distance	Reps	Time	Rest

COOL DOWN				
Activity	Distance	Reps	Time	Rest

TOTAL				

Date		Beginner ○	Intermediate ○	Advanced ○
Time				

WARM UP

Activity	Distance	Reps	Time	Rest

SETS

Activity	Distance	Reps	Time	Rest

COOL DOWN

Activity	Distance	Reps	Time	Rest

TOTAL				

Date	
Time	

Beginner ○   Intermediate ○   Advanced ○

WARM UP				
Activity	Distance	Reps	Time	Rest

SETS				
Activity	Distance	Reps	Time	Rest

COOL DOWN				
Activity	Distance	Reps	Time	Rest

TOTAL				

Date		
Time		

Beginner ○   Intermediate ○   Advanced ○

WARM UP				
Activity	Distance	Reps	Time	Rest

SETS				
Activity	Distance	Reps	Time	Rest

COOL DOWN				
Activity	Distance	Reps	Time	Rest

TOTAL				

Date	
Time	

Beginner ◯   Intermediate ◯   Advanced ◯

WARM UP				
Activity	Distance	Reps	Time	Rest

SETS				
Activity	Distance	Reps	Time	Rest

COOL DOWN				
Activity	Distance	Reps	Time	Rest

TOTAL				

Date		Beginner ○	Intermediate ○	Advanced ○
Time				

WARM UP				
Activity	**Distance**	**Reps**	**Time**	**Rest**

		SETS		
Activity	**Distance**	**Reps**	**Time**	**Rest**

		COOL DOWN		
Activity	**Distance**	**Reps**	**Time**	**Rest**

TOTAL				

Date	
Time	

Beginner ◯   Intermediate ◯   Advanced ◯

WARM UP				
Activity	Distance	Reps	Time	Rest

	SETS			
Activity	Distance	Reps	Time	Rest

		COOL DOWN		
Activity	Distance	Reps	Time	Rest

TOTAL				

Date					
Time					

Beginner ○   Intermediate ○   Advanced ○

WARM UP				
Activity	Distance	Reps	Time	Rest

	SETS			
Activity	Distance	Reps	Time	Rest

		COOL DOWN		
Activity	Distance	Reps	Time	Rest

TOTAL				

Date	
Time	

Beginner ◯   Intermediate ◯   Advanced ◯

WARM UP

Activity	Distance	Reps	Time	Rest

SETS

Activity	Distance	Reps	Time	Rest

COOL DOWN

Activity	Distance	Reps	Time	Rest

TOTAL				

Date	
Time	

Beginner ○   Intermediate ○   Advanced ○

WARM UP				
Activity	Distance	Reps	Time	Rest

	SETS			
Activity	Distance	Reps	Time	Rest

		COOL DOWN		
Activity	Distance	Reps	Time	Rest

TOTAL				

Date	
Time	

Beginner ⚪   Intermediate ⚪   Advanced ⚪

WARM UP

Activity	Distance	Reps	Time	Rest

SETS

Activity	Distance	Reps	Time	Rest

COOL DOWN

Activity	Distance	Reps	Time	Rest

TOTAL				

Date		Beginner ○	Intermediate ○	Advanced ○
Time				

WARM UP				
Activity	Distance	Reps	Time	Rest

SETS				
Activity	Distance	Reps	Time	Rest

COOL DOWN				
Activity	Distance	Reps	Time	Rest

TOTAL				

Date				
Time				

Beginner ◯   Intermediate ◯   Advanced ◯

WARM UP				
Activity	Distance	Reps	Time	Rest

SETS				
Activity	Distance	Reps	Time	Rest

COOL DOWN				
Activity	Distance	Reps	Time	Rest

TOTAL				

Date	
Time	

Beginner ○   Intermediate ○   Advanced ○

WARM UP

Activity	Distance	Reps	Time	Rest

SETS

Activity	Distance	Reps	Time	Rest

COOL DOWN

Activity	Distance	Reps	Time	Rest

TOTAL				

Date	
Time	

Beginner ○　　Intermediate ○　　Advanced ○

WARM UP				
Activity	**Distance**	**Reps**	**Time**	**Rest**

	SETS			
Activity	**Distance**	**Reps**	**Timc**	**Rest**

		COOL DOWN		
Activity	**Distance**	**Reps**	**Time**	**Rest**

TOTAL				

Date			Beginner ○	Intermediate ○	Advanced ○
Time					

WARM UP				
Activity	Distance	Reps	Time	Rest

SETS				
Activity	Distance	Reps	Time	Rest

		COOL DOWN		
Activity	Distance	Reps	Time	Rest

TOTAL				

Date	
Time	

Beginner ○   Intermediate ○   Advanced ○

WARM UP

Activity	Distance	Reps	Time	Rest

SETS

Activity	Distance	Reps	Time	Rest

COOL DOWN

Activity	Distance	Reps	Time	Rest

TOTAL				

Date		Beginner ⊙	Intermediate ⊙	Advanced ⊙
Time				

WARM UP				
Activity	Distance	Reps	Time	Rest

SETS				
Activity	Distance	Reps	Time	Rest

		COOL DOWN		
Activity	Distance	Reps	Time	Rest

TOTAL				

Date	
Time	

Beginner ◯   Intermediate ◯   Advanced ◯

WARM UP				
Activity	**Distance**	**Reps**	**Time**	**Rest**

	SETS			
Activity	**Distance**	**Reps**	**Time**	**Rest**

		COOL DOWN		
Activity	**Distance**	**Reps**	**Time**	**Rest**

TOTAL				

Date		Beginner ○	Intermediate ○	Advanced ○
Time				

WARM UP				
Activity	Distance	Reps	Time	Rest

	SETS			
Activity	Distance	Reps	Time	Rest

		COOL DOWN		
Activity	Distance	Reps	Time	Rest

TOTAL				

Date	
Time	

Beginner ○   Intermediate ○   Advanced ○

WARM UP				
Activity	**Distance**	**Reps**	**Time**	**Rest**

		SETS		
Activity	**Distance**	**Reps**	**Time**	**Rest**

		COOL DOWN		
Activity	**Distance**	**Reps**	**Time**	**Rest**

	TOTAL			

Date	
Time	

Beginner ⃝   Intermediate ⃝   Advanced ⃝

WARM UP				
Activity	**Distance**	**Reps**	**Time**	**Rest**

SETS				
Activity	**Distance**	**Reps**	**Time**	**Rest**

COOL DOWN				
Activity	**Distance**	**Reps**	**Time**	**Rest**

TOTAL				

Date	
Time	

Beginner ○   Intermediate ○   Advanced ○

WARM UP				
Activity	Distance	Reps	Time	Rest

SETS				
Activity	Distance	Reps	Time	Rest

COOL DOWN				
Activity	Distance	Reps	Time	Rest

TOTAL				

Date		Beginner ○	Intermediate ○	Advanced ○
Time				

WARM UP				
Activity	Distance	Reps	Time	Rest

SETS				
Activity	Distance	Reps	Time	Rest

COOL DOWN				
Activity	Distance	Reps	Time	Rest

TOTAL				

Date	
Time	

Beginner ◯   Intermediate ◯   Advanced ◯

WARM UP				
Activity	**Distance**	**Reps**	**Time**	**Rest**

SETS				
Activity	**Distance**	**Reps**	**Time**	**Rest**

			COOL DOWN	
Activity	**Distance**	**Reps**	**Time**	**Rest**

TOTAL				

Date	
Time	

Beginner ○   Intermediate ○   Advanced ○

WARM UP				
Activity	Distance	Reps	Time	Rest

SETS				
Activity	Distance	Reps	Time	Rest

		COOL DOWN		
Activity	Distance	Reps	Time	Rest

TOTAL				

Date	
Time	

Beginner ○   Intermediate ○   Advanced ○

WARM UP				
Activity	Distance	Reps	Time	Rest

		SETS		
Activity	Distance	Reps	Time	Rest

		COOL DOWN		
Activity	Distance	Reps	Time	Rest

TOTAL				

Date				
Time				

Beginner ○   Intermediate ○   Advanced ○

WARM UP				
Activity	Distance	Reps	Time	Rest

SETS				
Activity	Distance	Reps	Time	Rest

COOL DOWN				
Activity	Distance	Reps	Time	Rest

TOTAL				

Date	
Time	

Beginner ○   Intermediate ○   Advanced ○

WARM UP

Activity	Distance	Reps	Time	Rest

SETS

Activity	Distance	Reps	Time	Rest

COOL DOWN

Activity	Distance	Reps	Time	Rest

TOTAL				

Date			Beginner ◯	Intermediate ◯	Advanced ◯
Time					

WARM UP				
Activity	Distance	Reps	Time	Rest

		SETS		
Activity	Distance	Reps	Time	Rest

		COOL DOWN		
Activity	Distance	Reps	Time	Rest

TOTAL				

Date		Beginner ○	Intermediate ○	Advanced ○
Time				

WARM UP				
Activity	Distance	Reps	Time	Rest

		SETS		
Activity	Distance	Reps	Time	Rest

			COOL DOWN	
Activity	Distance	Reps	Time	Rest

TOTAL				

| Date | | Beginner ○ | Intermediate ○ | Advanced ○ |
| Time | | | | |

WARM UP				
Activity	Distance	Reps	Time	Rest

SETS				
Activity	Distance	Reps	Time	Rest

COOL DOWN				
Activity	Distance	Reps	Time	Rest

TOTAL				

Date				
Time				

Beginner ◯   Intermediate ◯   Advanced ◯

WARM UP				
Activity	Distance	Reps	Time	Rest

		SETS		
Activity	Distance	Reps	Time	Rest

			COOL DOWN	
Activity	Distance	Reps	Time	Rest

TOTAL				

Date				
Time				

Beginner ○   Intermediate ○   Advanced ○

WARM UP				
Activity	Distance	Reps	Time	Rest

		SETS		
Activity	Distance	Reps	Time	Rest

		COOL DOWN		
Activity	Distance	Reps	Time	Rest

TOTAL				

Date	
Time	

Beginner ◯   Intermediate ◯   Advanced ◯

WARM UP

Activity	Distance	Reps	Time	Rest

SETS

Activity	Distance	Reps	Time	Rest

COOL DOWN

Activity	Distance	Reps	Time	Rest

TOTAL				

Date					
Time		Beginner ○	Intermediate ○	Advanced ○	

WARM UP				
Activity	Distance	Reps	Time	Rest

SETS				
Activity	Distance	Reps	Time	Rest

COOL DOWN				
Activity	Distance	Reps	Time	Rest

TOTAL				

Date	
Time	

Beginner ○   Intermediate ○   Advanced ○

WARM UP				
Activity	Distance	Reps	Time	Rest

	SETS			
Activity	Distance	Reps	Time	Rest

		COOL DOWN		
Activity	Distance	Reps	Time	Rest

TOTAL				

61

Date	
Time	

Beginner ○   Intermediate ○   Advanced ○

WARM UP				
Activity	Distance	Reps	Time	Rest

SETS				
Activity	Distance	Reps	Time	Rest

COOL DOWN				
Activity	Distance	Reps	Time	Rest

TOTAL				

Date	
Time	

Beginner ○   Intermediate ○   Advanced ○

WARM UP				
Activity	Distance	Reps	Time	Rest

	SETS			
Activity	Distance	Reps	Time	Rest

		COOL DOWN		
Activity	Distance	Reps	Time	Rest

TOTAL				

Date				
Time				

Beginner ○   Intermediate ○   Advanced ○

WARM UP				
Activity	**Distance**	**Reps**	**Time**	**Rest**

SETS				
Activity	**Distance**	**Reps**	**Time**	**Rest**

		COOL DOWN		
Activity	**Distance**	**Reps**	**Time**	**Rest**

TOTAL				

Date	
Time	

Beginner ○   Intermediate ○   Advanced ○

WARM UP

Activity	Distance	Reps	Time	Rest

SETS

Activity	Distance	Reps	Time	Rest

COOL DOWN

Activity	Distance	Reps	Time	Rest

TOTAL				

Date		Beginner ○	Intermediate ○	Advanced ○
Time				

WARM UP				
Activity	Distance	Reps	Time	Rest

		SETS		
Activity	Distance	Reps	Time	Rest

			COOL DOWN	
Activity	Distance	Reps	Time	Rest

TOTAL				

Date	
Time	

Beginner ○   Intermediate ○   Advanced ○

WARM UP

Activity	Distance	Reps	Time	Rest

SETS

Activity	Distance	Reps	Time	Rest

COOL DOWN

Activity	Distance	Reps	Time	Rest

TOTAL				

Date		Beginner ⭕	Intermediate ⭕	Advanced ⭕
Time				

WARM UP				
Activity	Distance	Reps	Time	Rest

SETS				
Activity	Distance	Reps	Time	Rest

		COOL DOWN		
Activity	Distance	Reps	Time	Rest

TOTAL				

Date	
Time	

Beginner ○   Intermediate ○   Advanced ○

WARM UP				
Activity	Distance	Reps	Time	Rest

SETS				
Activity	Distance	Reps	Time	Rest

COOL DOWN				
Activity	Distance	Reps	Time	Rest

TOTAL				

Date	
Time	

Beginner ○ Intermediate ○ Advanced ○

WARM UP				
Activity	Distance	Reps	Time	Rest

SETS				
Activity	Distance	Reps	Time	Rest

		COOL DOWN		
Activity	Distance	Reps	Time	Rest

TOTAL				

70

Date	
Time	

Beginner ◯   Intermediate ◯   Advanced ◯

WARM UP				
Activity	Distance	Reps	Time	Rest

SETS				
Activity	Distance	Reps	Time	Rest

COOL DOWN				
Activity	Distance	Reps	Time	Rest

TOTAL				

| Date | | Beginner ○ | Intermediate ○ | Advanced ○ |
| Time | | | | |

WARM UP				
Activity	Distance	Reps	Time	Rest

		SETS		
Activity	Distance	Reps	Time	Rest

		COOL DOWN		
Activity	Distance	Reps	Time	Rest

TOTAL				

Date		Beginner ○	Intermediate ○	Advanced ○
Time				

WARM UP

Activity	Distance	Reps	Time	Rest

SETS

Activity	Distance	Reps	Time	Rest

COOL DOWN

Activity	Distance	Reps	Time	Rest

TOTAL				

Date				
Time		Beginner ○	Intermediate ○	Advanced ○

WARM UP				
Activity	Distance	Reps	Time	Rest

SETS				
Activity	Distance	Reps	Time	Rest

COOL DOWN				
Activity	Distance	Reps	Time	Rest

TOTAL				

Date	
Time	

Beginner ○   Intermediate ○   Advanced ○

WARM UP				
Activity	Distance	Reps	Time	Rest

	SETS			
Activity	Distance	Reps	Time	Rest

		COOL DOWN		
Activity	Distance	Reps	Time	Rest

	TOTAL			

Date				
Time				

Beginner ◯   Intermediate ◯   Advanced ◯

WARM UP				
Activity	**Distance**	**Reps**	**Time**	**Rest**

	SETS			
Activity	**Distance**	**Reps**	**Time**	**Rest**

		COOL DOWN		
Activity	**Distance**	**Reps**	**Time**	**Rest**

TOTAL				

Date	
Time	

Beginner ⚪   Intermediate ⚪   Advanced ⚪

WARM UP

Activity	Distance	Reps	Time	Rest

SETS

Activity	Distance	Reps	Time	Rest

COOL DOWN

Activity	Distance	Reps	Time	Rest

TOTAL				

Date		Beginner ○	Intermediate ○	Advanced ○
Time				

WARM UP

Activity	Distance	Reps	Time	Rest

SETS

Activity	Distance	Reps	Time	Rest

COOL DOWN

Activity	Distance	Reps	Time	Rest

TOTAL				

Date	
Time	

Beginner ◯   Intermediate ◯   Advanced ◯

WARM UP				
Activity	Distance	Reps	Time	Rest

	SETS			
Activity	Distance	Reps	Time	Rest

		COOL DOWN		
Activity	Distance	Reps	Time	Rest

TOTAL				

Date					
Time					

Beginner ○   Intermediate ○   Advanced ○

WARM UP					
Activity		**Distance**	**Reps**	**Time**	**Rest**

SETS					
Activity		**Distance**	**Reps**	**Time**	**Rest**

COOL DOWN					
Activity		**Distance**	**Reps**	**Time**	**Rest**

TOTAL					

Date	
Time	

Beginner ○   Intermediate ○   Advanced ○

WARM UP				
Activity	Distance	Reps	Time	Rest

SETS				
Activity	Distance	Reps	Time	Rest

COOL DOWN				
Activity	Distance	Reps	Time	Rest

TOTAL				

Date	
Time	

Beginner ○   Intermediate ○   Advanced ○

WARM UP				
Activity	**Distance**	**Reps**	**Time**	**Rest**

	SETS			
Activity	**Distance**	**Reps**	**Time**	**Rest**

		COOL DOWN		
Activity	**Distance**	**Reps**	**Time**	**Rest**

TOTAL			

Date				
Time				

Beginner ○   Intermediate ○   Advanced ○

WARM UP

Activity	Distance	Reps	Time	Rest

SETS

Activity	Distance	Reps	Time	Rest

COOL DOWN

Activity	Distance	Reps	Time	Rest

TOTAL				

Date				
Time				

Beginner ○   Intermediate ○   Advanced ○

WARM UP				
Activity	Distance	Reps	Time	Rest

	SETS			
Activity	Distance	Reps	Time	Rest

		COOL DOWN		
Activity	Distance	Reps	Time	Rest

TOTAL				

Date					
Time					

Beginner ◯   Intermediate ◯   Advanced ◯

WARM UP					
Activity	Distance	Reps	Time	Rest

SETS					
Activity	Distance	Reps	Time	Rest

COOL DOWN					
Activity	Distance	Reps	Time	Rest

TOTAL				

Date				
Time		Beginner ⚪	Intermediate ⚪	Advanced ⚪

WARM UP				
Activity	Distance	Reps	Time	Rest

SETS				
Activity	Distance	Reps	Time	Rest

COOL DOWN				
Activity	Distance	Reps	Time	Rest

TOTAL				

Date	
Time	

Beginner ○   Intermediate ○   Advanced ○

WARM UP				
Activity	Distance	Reps	Time	Rest

	SETS			
Activity	Distance	Reps	Time	Rest

			COOL DOWN	
Activity	Distance	Reps	Time	Rest

TOTAL				

| Date | | Beginner ○ | Intermediate ○ | Advanced ○ |
| Time | | | | |

WARM UP

Activity	Distance	Reps	Time	Rest

SETS

Activity	Distance	Reps	Time	Rest

COOL DOWN

Activity	Distance	Reps	Time	Rest

TOTAL				

Date	
Time	

Beginner ○   Intermediate ○   Advanced ○

WARM UP

Activity	Distance	Reps	Time	Rest

SETS

Activity	Distance	Reps	Time	Rest

COOL DOWN

Activity	Distance	Reps	Time	Rest

TOTAL				

| Date | | Beginner ○ | Intermediate ○ | Advanced ○ |
| Time | | | | |

WARM UP				
Activity	Distance	Reps	Time	Rest

	SETS			
Activity	Distance	Reps	Time	Rest

		COOL DOWN		
Activity	Distance	Reps	Time	Rest

| TOTAL | | | | |

Date	
Time	

Beginner ◯   Intermediate ◯   Advanced ◯

WARM UP

Activity	Distance	Reps	Time	Rest

SETS

Activity	Distance	Reps	Time	Rest

COOL DOWN

Activity	Distance	Reps	Time	Rest

TOTAL				

Date	
Time	

Beginner ○   Intermediate ○   Advanced ○

WARM UP				
Activity	Distance	Reps	Time	Rest

SETS				
Activity	Distance	Reps	Time	Rest

COOL DOWN				
Activity	Distance	Reps	Time	Rest

TOTAL				

Date	
Time	

Beginner ○ Intermediate ○ Advanced ○

WARM UP				
Activity	Distance	Reps	Time	Rest

	SETS			
Activity	Distance	Reps	Time	Rest

		COOL DOWN		
Activity	Distance	Reps	Time	Rest

TOTAL				

Date	
Time	

Beginner ⃝   Intermediate ⃝   Advanced ⃝

WARM UP				
Activity	Distance	Reps	Time	Rest

SETS				
Activity	Distance	Reps	Time	Rest

		COOL DOWN		
Activity	Distance	Reps	Time	Rest

TOTAL				

Date	
Time	

Beginner ○   Intermediate ○   Advanced ○

WARM UP				
Activity	Distance	Reps	Time	Rest

SETS				
Activity	Distance	Reps	Time	Rest

		COOL DOWN		
Activity	Distance	Reps	Time	Rest

TOTAL				

95

Date			
Time			

Beginner ○   Intermediate ○   Advanced ○

WARM UP				
Activity	Distance	Reps	Time	Rest

SETS				
Activity	Distance	Reps	Time	Rest

COOL DOWN				
Activity	Distance	Reps	Time	Rest

TOTAL				

Date		Beginner ◯	Intermediate ◯	Advanced ◯
Time				

WARM UP				
Activity	**Distance**	**Reps**	**Time**	**Rest**

		SETS		
Activity	**Distance**	**Reps**	**Time**	**Rest**

		COOL DOWN		
Activity	**Distance**	**Reps**	**Time**	**Rest**

TOTAL				

Date		Beginner ◯	Intermediate ◯	Advanced ◯
Time				

WARM UP				
Activity	Distance	Reps	Time	Rest

SETS				
Activity	Distance	Reps	Time	Rest

COOL DOWN				
Activity	Distance	Reps	Time	Rest

TOTAL				

Date		Beginner ◯	Intermediate ◯	Advanced ◯
Time				

WARM UP					
	Activity	Distance	Reps	Time	Rest

		SETS			
	Activity	Distance	Reps	Time	Rest

			COOL DOWN		
	Activity	Distance	Reps	Time	Rest

TOTAL				

Date	
Time	

Beginner ◯　　Intermediate ◯　　Advanced ◯

WARM UP				
Activity	Distance	Reps	Time	Rest

SETS				
Activity	Distance	Reps	Time	Rest

COOL DOWN				
Activity	Distance	Reps	Time	Rest

TOTAL				

Date				
Time				

Beginner ◯   Intermediate ◯   Advanced ◯

WARM UP				
Activity	Distance	Reps	Time	Rest

SETS				
Activity	Distance	Reps	Time	Rest

		COOL DOWN		
Activity	Distance	Reps	Time	Rest

TOTAL				

Made in the USA
Las Vegas, NV
16 August 2022

53362850R00069